Pra

Guardian Angel

By
REV. LAWRENCE G. LOVASIK, S.V.D.
Divine Word Missionary

NIHIL OBSTAT: Rev. James M. Cafone, M.A., S.T.D., Censor Librorum
IMPRIMATUR: ✠ Most Rev. John J. Myers, D.D., J.C.D., Archbishop of Newark

The Nihil Obstat and Imprimatur are official declarations that a book or pamphlet is free of doctrinal or moral error. No implication is contained therein that those who have granted the Nihil Obstat and Imprimatur agree with the contents, opinions or statements expressed.

Printed in Hong Kong   ISBN 978-0-89942-529-0

PRAYER TO MY MESSENGER FROM GOD

DEAR Guardian Angel,
God made you with no body.
That makes you a spirit.

Although I have never seen you,
I know that you are always with me.

You stand alongside me,
protecting me from harm,
and showing me how to be
faithful to God.

Thank you for being my
own messenger from God.

PRAYER TO
MY EVERLASTING FRIEND

DEAR Guardian Angel,
Jesus knew how important
you would be in my life,
and in the lives of all children.

He even told His Apostles
to become like little children
and never to harm little ones like me.

Jesus knew that children's
Angels in heaven
always see the face of God,
our Father.

Thank you for protecting me
as you watch from heaven above.

PRAYER TO MY CONSTANT COMPANION

DEAR Guardian Angel,
when I was born,
God sent you to watch over me
all the days of my life.

You truly are my protector,
my special helper,
my constant companion,
my everlasting friend.

Thank you for always being
so many things to me,
even if I may not always think of you
or if I take you for granted.

PRAYER TO MY
SPECIAL HELPER

DEAR Guardian Angel,
you know the great joy
of loving and serving God.

I, too, want to love God
and serve Him every day.

With your help,
I will please God
with my thoughts,
with my speech,
and with my actions.

Thank you for showing me the way.

9

PRAYER TO
MY PROTECTOR

DEAR Guardian Angel,
there are many ways
that harm can find its way to me.

I know that danger can sometimes
appear out of nowhere.

But I feel safe and embraced
by your protection.

I know that you watch over both
my body and my soul.

Thank you for your watchful care,
and for taking seriously
your responsibility to guard me.

PRAYER OF APPRECIATION

DEAR Guardian Angel,
you help me appreciate
all that God has made.

You help me smell
the sweetness of the flowers.

You help me feel
the warmth of the sunshine.

You help me to be happy
when I hear the birds chirping.

Thank you for making my senses
more aware of all around me.

PRAYER FOR FAMILY LOVE

DEAR Guardian Angel,
you help me to know
that God loves me
and wants me to be happy.

You help me to share that love
with my parents and my siblings.

When I talk back to my mom or dad
or am mean to my brother or sister,
remind me of my special love for them.

Thank you for helping me
to love my family each day.

PRAYER FOR KINDNESS

DEAR Guardian Angel,
you help me realize
that I make Jesus happy
when I am kind to others.

I hear your whispers in my heart,
reminding me to be kind—
to my schoolmates,
to my friends,
even to people I may not like.

Thank you for showing me
how important it is
to be kind always.

PRAYER FOR SHARING

DEAR Guardian Angel,
you know how many blessings
God has given me.

Besides my family,
I have a home, warm clothes,
good food, and toys.

Some children may have more,
but many have far less.

Thank you for helping me
not to take for granted what I have
and encouraging me
to share with others
whenever possible.

PRAYER FOR
THOUGHTS OF GOD

DEAR Guardian Angel,
how lucky you are to be
in God's presence always.

He is ever in your thoughts
because you are there with Him.

I often am busy with all kinds of activities—
school, sports, practices,
television, video games, computers.

With all there is to do,
sometimes I forget about God.

Thank you for reminding me
to stop and think about God
and all He means to me.

PRAYER TO
OPEN MY HEART

DEAR Guardian Angel,
you do so much for me.
One of the best things is
that you pray for me.

And, even more,
you help me to pray.

With each day,
help me to pray better.
Help me not always to ask for something,
but to thank God and praise Him instead.

Thank you for this special help
to show God how much I love Him.

PRAYER FOR OBEDIENCE

DEAR Guardian Angel,
you help me realize how much
my mom and dad love me,
and how they want only
what is good for me.

By obeying them,
I keep the Fourth Commandment.

I honor them,
and I show them my love.

Thank you for encouraging me
to obey them in all things—
big and small.

PRAYER FOR
LOVE OF JESUS

DEAR Guardian Angel,
I know that Jesus loves me,
but I may not always show
my love for Him.

With your help,
I will work to be more grateful,
to be kinder to others,
to share myself and my gifts,
to pray better each day,
and to be more obedient.

Thank you for standing by me as I try
in all these ways to show Jesus my love.

PRAYER FOR
PEACEFUL SLEEP

DEAR Guardian Angel,
when my busy day is over,
you are still beside me.

Although I am tired,
you remain ever watchful,
even as I sleep.

You make me feel safe,
and I have no fears or worries.

Thank you for all your days with me
and for all nights that are peaceful
because you are with me.

PRAYER OF LOVE

DEAR Guardian Angel,
please help me to remember
how special you are to me.

You help me to face each day
with faith in God.

You help me to face each day
with hope in what I can be.

You help me face each day
with love for others.

I thank you and I love you
for all your gifts each day.

PRAYER TO
MY GUARDIAN ANGEL

ANGEL of God,
my Guardian dear,
God's love for me
has sent you here.

Ever this day
be at my side,
to light and guard,
to rule and guide.